# Catch That Phrase
## *A Message Within A Message*

"WOW!!!!! GOOD NIGHT!!!!!! THIS IS A BIG ONE!!!!!!!"

# BRENDA T. RICE

**Illustrations by
Tiffany Taylor and
Brenda Rice**

iUniverse LLC
Bloomington

Catch That Phrase
A Message Within A Message

Copyright © 2011, 2013 Brenda T. Rice

iUniverse books may be ordered through booksellers or by contacting:

iUniverse LLC
1663 Liberty Drive
Bloomington, IN 47403
www.iuniverse.com
1-800-Authors (1-800-288-4677)

Because of the dynamic nature of the Internet, any Web addresses or
links contained in this book may have changed since publication and
may no longer be valid. The views expressed in this work are solely those
of the author and do not necessarily reflect the views of the publisher,
and the publisher hereby disclaims any responsibility for them.

Any people depicted in stock imagery provided by Thinkstock are models,
and such images are being used for illustrative purposes only.

Certain stock imagery © Thinkstock.

ISBN: 978-1-4502-6842-4 (sc)
ISBN: 978-1-4620-1069-1 (e)

Printed in the United States of America

iUniverse rev. date: 11/25/2013

BRENDA T. RICE is a resident and native of Henderson, N.C. She is the daughter of Mary Stovall. She is a graduate from Vance Senior High in Henderson and graduated with a B.A. degree in Mass Communications with a minor in Art Appreciation from Shaw University in Raleigh, N.C. Prior to Shaw she attended Alamance Community College in Burlington, N.C., where she studied one year in Art and Audio Visual Aides. She is married to Pastor Seamon Rice, Jr.; they are the proud parents of three wonderful adults, Crystal, Michael and Jonathan.

Rice's commitment to Christian service includes Preacher, Worship Leader and Bible Study Teacher. She served as Youth Missionary Advisor at Big Ruin Creek Baptist Church and for the Vance County Missionary Union. And also held an office in the Young Adult Department of the Women's Home Foreign Missionary Convention of North Carolina, Inc. Her love for missions has allowed her ministry to expand outside of the US to several foreign countries which includes Oaxaca, Mexico, Mumbai, India, Guyana, South America, Nigeria, West Africa and Nelspruit, South Africa.

She is actively involved in the ministry at New Covenant Faith (Henderson, N.C.) where her husband serves as Pastor. *Brenda continues to share the message of hope and inspiration (through singing and preaching God's word) in her community and throughout the world with love and dedication.*

# Foreword

Catch Phrases - tell me who doesn't use them? I grew up on catch phrases or as some may use them as plain common sense words. I am happy to have this wonderful opportunity to give expressions about the book, "Catch That Phrase", that my friend Minister Brenda Rice has written for your enjoyment.

In this book, Minister Brenda Rice focuses on phrases that she was inspired to write and use; as well as some familiar and modern phrases heard from family, friends, in sermons, or in general conversations. Catch Phrases are a part of everyday life. For example, a couple I've heard and use today- "It's a good day for ducks!"(on a rainy day), and "Hold on wait!"(for when I feel as if I'm rushed by someone).

I hope that you purchase this book and read it, not only read, but enjoy what you are reading. Enjoy reading the cute, funny and sometime serious catch phrases that Minister Rice shares with us. I'm sure that you will find complete enjoyment and words of wisdom that are found in these catch phrases.

*Linda Crews*

*"As the vision unfolds hear the mysteries untold."*

Pastor Seamon Rice

"Appreciate the Past, Celebrate where you are, Evaluate your offsets, Concentrate on moving forward, Participate in the process, Anticipate your Success."

Brenda T. Rice

# Why This Book

This book is so exciting. It is a collection of quotes and phrases gathered from family, friends and myself that can often be meaningful in our lives. The statement is true one word spoken in a person's life can do one of two things, make you or break you. The reason I was inspired to do this book is my love for short catch phrases. I've used them in my own life and passed them on to our children. I was so fascinated by the sayings of others I started writing down as many as I could; some are funny but keep you focused, others are serious but lead to improving lives.

I wanted to share these inspirational sayings to encourage the reader. The phrases in this book are few in words but they are powerful and meaningful with a lasting effect. If one or more of these quotes (sayings) can help you then I've fulfilled the reason for being inspired to write this book. I suggest that you use them daily to motivate you, highlight those that really fit you, and write them down. The more you use them, the more they will be apart of who you are. CATCH THAT PHRASE AND KEEP IT!!!!!

I would like to dedicate this book to:

my mother Mary Stovall;

my father in law Deacon Seamon Rice, Sr.

my husband Pastor Seamon Rice, Jr.

my children, Crystal, Michael, and Jonathan

my sisters and brothers and other relatives

and friends

*Thank God*

*Special Thanks*

*Crystal Rice, Lesia Rice, Linda Crews, Whitney McGee, Justin Davis, Linda Taylor, Tiffany Taylor, Francine Burwell, Kimberly Smith, Michael Rice*

*"Celebrate those who celebrate you."*

*Brenda Rice*

*"Turn your mourning into dancing."*

*"A gift is as a precious stone in the eyes of him that hath it: wheresoever it turneth it prospereth."*

**(Proverbs 17:8)**

*"Hope deferred maketh the heart sick: but when the desire cometh, it is a tree of life."*

**(Proverb 13:12)**

*"What you behold is what you become,*
*behold Jesus."*

*"Get right or get left!"*

*"Sleep leads to poverty but prayer leads to prosperity."*

*"I feel God and I fear God!"*

*"When you change the way man thinks, you change the man."*

*"Get Up!! And get to mo-vin!!!"*

*"You got to see yourself out before you come out."*

*"Let peace be the empire of your soul."*

◊

*"Don't speak about it be about it!"*

◊

*"My focus is not broken."*

◊

*"Justified by faith, living under grace, walking by faith."*

◊

*"In certain situations, It's not what happens
to you, it's how you handle it."*

◊

*"Heavy but heartfelt."*

◊

*"God can fix this!"*

*"Wonderful…have a wonderful day!"*

◊

*"Anybody Excited!"*

◊

*"Watch Yourself!"*

◊

*"What the world!"*

◊

*"You better help somebody!"*

◊

*"Praise the Lord, I am blessed and highly favored!"*

◊

*"Your desire is your destiny."*

◊

*"Catch on fire to ignite the hearts of men."*

*"You can't fix what you are unwilling to face."*

Personal Journal

_____

_____

_____

_____

_____

_____

_____

_____

_____

_____

_____

_____

_____

_____

_____

_____

_____

_____

_____

_____

_____

_____

_____

*"Be prayerfully careful."*

*"When will you stop giving lip service?"*

◊

*"Make the best of every situation."*

◊

*"If you want  something done—then you see that it's done."*

◊

*"Where do you go from where you presently are?"*

◊

*"Be aware of the negative whispers."*

◊

*"It's time to step up to the plate and do something."*

◊

*"Expect nothing, get nothing."*

◊

*"Give good!!! Get good!"*

◊

*"Everybody in a hurry going nowhere."*

*"Seven days without prayer makes one weak."*

*"This is ch—ch what's missing?"*

*"You don't have to be great to begin you have to begin to be great."*

*"Men are not attracted to women of power but women are attracted to men of power."*

*"I'm tired of expecting, its time for my deliverance."*

*God said," if you walk it out then I'll work it out."*

*"Seasoning is for flavoring food; God wants us to season the earth."*

"In *the midst of the turbulence I'm moving in the right direction.*"

"*Don't spend all your time talking to God but allow God to talk back to you.*"

"*We are evolving, we are ever changing.*"

"*You came in this earth at the time of your birth don't leave till you complete your task.*"

"*In order to have good character you must follow good principles.*"

"*A true friend will tell you the truth.*"

"*Trials and tribulations are the fertilizer that helps us grow.*"

Ocean's View

By Tiffany Taylor

*"I was made to give the Lord the praise!"*

*"If you don't expect it you won't get it."*

Personal Journal

_____

_____

_____

_____

_____

_____

_____

_____

_____

_____

_____

_____

_____

_____

_____

_____

_____

_____

_____

_____

_____

_____

_____

*"If you didn't plant corn on that row
then don't expect corn to grow."*

*Honey child," If you just think then you will be thankful!"*

*"When you make yourself available;
God will make you capable."*

*"You are on the battlefield with a playground mentality."*

*"Are you the concrete to someone's abstract?"*

◊

"Hold Steady!"

◊

*"Watch whose watching you."*

◊

*"Obtain!!!!!! And Maintain!!!!"*

*"If you can't do it yourself then get you some help."*

*"Don't speak it———do it!"*

*"Yes!!!!!!! My Lord."*

*"Blessings on you!"*

*"When you think you have failed; you are not a failure. Be willing to start again."*

*"Oh!!!!! Father!"*

*"When you have done all you know, get some help."*

*"Sometime the reward is greater than the pain."*

*"It is better to have it and not need it than to need it and not have it."*

*"Be ready to fight on the journey."*

◊

*"Lord, show up and show out!"*

◊

*"Operate from Revelation not just Information."*

◊

*"When you limit God to the possibilities of man you limit God."*

◊

*"If you never had challenges then you will never grow."*

◊

"I *am going to do my best and let God do the rest."*

◊

*"Time will leave yo' behind!"*

◊

*"Age is a state of time; old is a state of mind."*

*"Don 't just breakout but breakout with focus."*

*"Admit it and quit it!"*

*"You make me cry (not sad) but you also make me smile."*

*"It's not how you begin, it's really how you end."*

*"The seed you sow is the seed that grow!"*

*"A set up for my step up."*

*"You have to think you are somebody even
when you feel like you are a nobody."*

## AIR BALLOONS

*"Always move in the direction of God."*

*"Follow me on Facebook!!! Get your face in the book (The Bible) and follow the Text…!" Pastor Seamon Rice*

Personal Journal

_____
_____
_____
_____
_____
_____
_____
_____
_____
_____
_____
_____
_____
_____
_____
_____
_____
_____
_____
_____
_____
_____
_____
_____

*"Aiming with your eyes closed hoping you will hit the mark!"*

*Peaceful*

*"Why is it that people notice what they need to do
but they won't take action?" Crystal Rice*

*"When you leave this world you are going by yourself anyway."*

*"It doesn 't take much to be a Christian, it takes
all. It doesn't take too much to be a sinner, it
takes all...Sins Robs, Kills and Destroys."*

*"If there is praying in the pew, there will
be preaching from the pulpit."*

*"I don't know when I lost it but I've got my grip back!"*

*"People can get comfortable in uncomfortable situations."*

*"You can try if you want to but you can't block my blessings."*

*"Check it and Change it!"*

"In *your lifetime you may not achieve everything, but achieve something worthwhile.*"

◊

"*Nobody will remember you for walking in shallow waters so take action and step out into the deep.*"

◊

"*Nothing should irritate or frustrate you so much to cause you to go backward but every irritation and frustration should push you forward into your destiny.*"

◊

"*Give a little bit more than you are getting.*"

◊

"*Don't hang around dummies.*"

◊

"*A good attitude can go along way.*"

◊

"*Being grown comes with responsibility and accountability.*"

◊

"*There can not be a breakthrough until there is a break forth.*"

*"Pray about everything worry about nothing."*

*"You can't lead the people if you are sleeping with the people."*

*"Just because you don't have it now doesn't
mean you are not going to get it."*

*"No matter how successful you become
never forget where you came from."*

*"The wider the door is opened, the responsibility may be greater."*

*"Time seems to go by faster when you are on your own time."*

*"God abides in all time at the same time."*

*"Things can happen when we all work together."*

Personal Journal

_____

_____

_____

_____

_____

_____

_____

_____

_____

_____

_____

_____

_____

_____

_____

_____

_____

_____

_____

_____

_____

_____

*"Give the Lord the maximum glory."*

*"The spiritual range of your soul provokes supernatural power."*

◊

*"Cheaper is not always better."*

◊

*"Before the shifting their must be a shaking."*

◊

*"When the inner (spiritual) man is energized
then the hu——man won't compromise."*

◊

*"God is so good to me better than I have a right to complain."*

◊

*"You have to see it before you have it and
you have to say it if you want it."*

◊

*God, "use me to the max!"*

◊

*"The word (the Bible) works when you work the word."*

◊

*"You cannot kick against prayer."*

*"Are you a go————————getter or are you a no—getter?"*

Brenda T. Rice

*"Just because you've experienced a loss, it still doesn't mean that you don't have the potential to win."*

Brenda T. Rice

*"Praise is what we do to come through."*

◊

*"God is on time, in time for such a time."*

◊

*"When you know what time it is, then you will know how to operate time."*

◊

*"The Devil is a liar because he left the truth."*

◊

*"Day by day you are drifting away."*

◊

*"Exceed what people expect of you."*

◊

*"Information!! Revelation!! Application!!"*

◊

*"Dreams and goals…Pursue the Process!!!! Making progress!!"*

Winter

*"Do the very best you can according to the situation you are in."*

*"Your praise should never be bankrupt; you should never have insufficient praise."*

Pastor Seamon Rice

*"Don't let the devil go messing with yo' blessing!"*

Brenda Rice

*"Some people are chasing after God and some are being chased by God."*

Personal Journal

_____

_____

_____

_____

_____

_____

_____

_____

_____

_____

_____

_____

_____

_____

_____

_____

_____

_____

_____

_____

_____

_____

_____

_____

_____

_____

_____

_____

*"Why ya acting like ya acting?"*

*"Letting your light shine is a lifestyle."*

◊

*"Not this week I'm sleep."*

◊

*"If you don't you won't"*

◊

*"We all need to be in self check mode."*

◊

*"Dreams, aspirations and inspirations
must be embraced and pursued."*

◊

*"Use your gifts and talents until you used them up."*

◊

*"You can't go back and get time but you can
take advantage of the present time."*

Nap Time
By Brenda Rice

*"You can lean on me whenever you want too."*

# A SISTER HUG

Brenda Rice

*"Expression of Love…"*

## Feature Sections

**Story Time Linda Taylor**

The Leader of the Pack

Being Different

My Father

**Poetry Korner Francine Burwell**

Let Jesus Weather Your Storm

Urgent Prayer

Purpose

**Michael Rice**

Success

Why

Drums

**Kimberly Smith**

Behind These Eyes

Wilderness Gone

Encouragement for Today

# STORY TIME
# By Linda Taylor

# The Leader of the Pack

This is a story about cats, all kinds of cats. They were cats of many shapes and colors, black, pink, and blue. Some of them were fat; some were skinny, big and small. There were so many cats until they decided that a leader was needed. So the black cat was appointed as leader among the group. A lot of cats would bow down to this black cat because he told them that he was the boss and they must listen to him. They didn't like this at all but they did it anyway.

One day while the boss was away with some of the others, one cat decided to go out to find a cat to help get them out of this mess. He found a beautiful white cat. While they were talking the white cat said "go back and tell them everything will be just fine". So the cat told them that everything would be fine but they thought he was crazy. They didn't believe he saw or even talked to a white cat.

It was late one night when the white cat appeared that they really believed. He was the most beautiful cat they'd ever seen. The cats all gathered around him; their eyes were wide open and everyone was talking and whispering. When you looked at him you felt nothing but peace, love and joy. The black cat saw this and began to wonder what was going on. So, he decided to go find out what the fuss was about. When he saw the white cat, he told him to step down because he was the boss. The white cat said, "there is no boss, you were chosen to be the leader because it was so many cats; not to boss them around. So no one should tell anybody what to do. We should work together and listen to one another regardless of what we look like or the color of our skin. If you are light, dark, red, pink or even white, it doesn't matter. We should all love one another.

# Being Different

This story is about a zebra that was much different from the others. He didn't have black and white strips but was filled with all the bright colors of the rainbow. This zebra was very sad because he didn't like being different. He tried washing the colors off with soap, water and covering himself with clay. When his mother saw what he was doing she sat him down and told him he should be happy because God made him special. He still couldn't understand why God made him so different. So one night he decided to leave home to find someone or something that looked like him. The zebra started walking until he saw a ranch. The ranch was filled with colorful animals but no zebras. He continued to walk down the road to a field of colorful flowers. They all were smiling at him but still no zebras. The day was getting darker and he was getting tired; so he found a very tall flower to lie under and fell asleep. While the zebra was sleeping a storm arose and he opened his eyes for a minute and then went back to sleep. After the storm was over the sunlight on his face caused him to awake. To his surprise; he saw a bright rainbow. He couldn't believe how beautiful a rainbow was with as many colors as himself. The zebra got up and decided to go home and told everyone what he had seen with his own eyes. He said. "God made the colors of the rainbow to show the beauty of this world and he gave me these beautiful colors to show how beautiful I am."

# My Father

My Father was born to a virgin named Mary. He brought a little girl back to life and was tempted by the devil in the wilderness. He healed a paralytic man and made a blind man see. My Father fed 5000 people with two fish and five loaves of bread. He loves children and all people. Do you know that the Chief Priest and Elders of the people decided to put my Father to death; someone betrayed him for money. The soldiers mocked Him; they stripped my Father and put a crown of thorns and placed it on His head. They mocked my Father and led Him to a tomb. But after three days he rose from the dead. I love my (Heavenly) Father and I am not ashamed. A lot of single mothers' tell their children that they don't have a father when the father is not around. But mothers should let them know about the heavenly Father. He's always there when you need Him. He's always around all through the week and on the weekend too. He loves you no mater what, he's never too busy for you. So children know this, you have a Father who sets high and looks low and he will be with you until the end. When you feel like no one cares, know that you can talk to the heavenly Father.

# POETRY KORNER
# By Francine Burwell

# Let Jesus Weather Your Storm

*Today's unknown forecast may call for many things whatever*
*the weather is just be prepared for what it brings*

*If it somehow calls for rain and mostly cloudy skies*
*Don't give up give in Sunshine is surely high*

*If a tornado quickly occurs*
*And all your troubles increase*
*Start speaking to your storm*
*And tell the winds to cease*

*But if ever a massive hurricane*
*Should send destruction your way*
*Stand boldly with the Master*
*And stop the waves at bay*

*Be on the lookout for blizzards your inheritance*
*it will freeze but speak those things in existence*
*and watch Him supply your need*

*No matter what type of storm*
*May decide to come your way*
*My Savior has the power*
*To make the storm obey*

# Urgent Prayer

*I had a situation that needed special care*
*So I fell on my knees and said a special prayer*

*I said "Dear Heavenly Father*
*I need your Help today*
*I need your spiritual guidance*
*I need it right away"*

*He said to me my child I know just what you need*
*I have all the answers if you just follow my lead*

*If you take a closer look*
*In me is what you 'll see I am greater than your*
*problem and there's nothing too hard for me*

*Your request has been known and the problem has been repaired*
*Thank you for the invitation Through the Urgency of your prayer*

# Purpose

*Have you ever sat and wondered what is the purpose*
*for my life? Is it to be a teacher, a lawyer?*
*Maybe a scientist and architect?*

*A pilot or engineer, I could imagine being an*
*accountant or having a military career,*

*An entrepreneur Um that some how sounds nice, I*
*could be my own boss and set my own pace.*

*Just think my purpose is reserved*
*for me to fulfill*
*only through my obedience to God*
*can it be revealed.*

*For God knows the plan and purpose for my life. The plan*
*to prosper me, not harm me, but to give me eternal life.*

*What good is trying to fulfill your purpose*
*without Jesus Christ? Because you will never tap into*
*destiny, without making the ultimate sacrifice.*

# POETRY KORNER
## By Michael Rice

# Define Success

*Success is a journey,*
*I write in my journal,*
*3o pages of successful plans,*
*That I plan to achieve,*
*My emotions are full of joy, happiness, and gladness,*
*Because I see myself building success,*
*It's like I'm building prosperous steps that will never end,*
*Pens running out of ink,*
*Because the race to success tends,*
*To test my personal motivation,*
*But I'm not afraid to ask for help,*
*Helps me see that I'm not the only one,*
*In it to win the game,*
*Of successful gains,*
*I gain skills by listening and learning,*
*Setting myself to be humble,*
*Cause I'm striving for more,*
*I'm dreaming of it,*
*Walking down future road,*
*As I stop at the crossroad,*
*I see 4 big signs say,*
*Success*
*I define my Success can u see yours?*

# Why

*Why is always the question?*
*Suggesting why I should,*
*Believe that the days I would,*
*Be living is the best days ahead of me,*
*But a head are stumble rocks and road blocks,*
*That's brings me back to the question*
*Why?*
*Why spell backwards is confusing,*
*And in my mind I'm confuse cause what I thought was so close,*
*Is so far away,*
*In ways I'm beginning to shrug my shoulders because I just don't*
*know*
*Why?*
*But Wait what's that?*
*A light, a light that shines so bright*
*Right through my dark clouds,*
*This light is Life,*
*That brings me back to the question,*
*But I know what life is; now I know WHY!!!*

# Drums

*I can hear a nice warm rhythm, the heat from my soul,*
*Drives my hands and feet the cry from the cymbals,*
*Sends a chill down my spine,*
*I find joy when I hear that sound,*
*The stroke from hitting the snare and Tums,*
*Controls the air,*
*Sending echo's off the wall,*
*All I see is my wrist in motion,*
*Moving like waves in the ocean,*
*I can see this is my passion,*
*My leg sends power to the bass beat,*
*Making it hard for me to stay in my seat,*
*Sitting down in front of this my comfort zone,*
*Putting these tunes on my ring tone,*
*Sound like a ticking time bomb,*
*I'm doing what I love,*
*Playing the DRUMS!!!!!*

Corner Street Harmonizers

*"Don't hate or under estimate but appreciate
and celebrate the power of God."*

Michael Rice

*"It pays to be kind…even when it doesn't come
from the one you showed kindness too."*

Personal Journal

_____
_____
_____
_____
_____
_____
_____
_____
_____
_____
_____
_____
_____
_____
_____
_____
_____
_____
_____
_____
_____
_____
_____

*"Don't count me out because I'm in for the count down."*

# POETRY KORNER
# By Kimberly L. Smith

# Behind These Eyes

*Behind these eyes*
There's a story to tell
A story of pain, hurt and loss
A story hidden so well

*Behind these eyes* Lies the memories from a mountain of mess
Though memories are clear the thing
much clearer is your deliverance

*Deliverance* from the things that
Could have killed me
Could have demolished my sanity
Could have warped my way of thinking
Could have taken away my God given ability to love
Could have caused hate to be my second name
*Deliverance ... Oh God, Your Deliverance!*

*Behind these eyes*
There's a story to tell
Of divine strength, character and courage
Of unbendable faith
Of undeniable love
Of unquestionable trust

*Behind these eyes*
*behind these eyes*

# Encouragement for Today

*Lift up your heads, O ye gates; and be ye lift up, ye everlasting doors; and the King of glory shall come in. @ (Psalm 24:7 KJV)*

**In** *other words, the King, the True Captain will come in to lift you up. To gently touch your face and say, lift your head up daughter; lift your head up son. I chose you. I chose you for My team.*

*There is no greater honor than to be chosen by Me and to be placed on My team. For on My team there is unlimited love and continual acceptance of you My child. On My team I will hold your hand and I will give you direction. I will never leave you and I will never forsake you. I will be that support that you will constantly need in your life.*

*You will never know rejection coming from me and you will never have to wonder if I chose you as a last resort. I chose you because you were made in my likeness. You are a part of me, taken from my very own heartbeat.*

**Don't ever forget that God chose you and that He loves you just as you are. *Nothing will ever change His love for you.***

Copyright © 2004 by Kimberly L. Smith

# Wilderness Gone

You don't understand

You don't understand

I passed the test

I don't have to walk around in that wilderness Anymore

The lessons to be learned I learned them

The stories to be told I told them

The prayers to be prayed I prayed them

The songs to be sung I sang them

The tears to be cried I cried them, *oh I cried them*

*But, oh the joy to be felt I felt it*

The day I realized that wilderness ... that
particular wilderness is not for me Anymore!

Copyright 8 7/25/03 by Kimberly L. Smith

*"If you get it in your mind you will have it every time."*

Personal Journal

_____

_____

_____

_____

_____

_____

_____

_____

_____

_____

_____

_____

_____

_____

_____

_____

_____

_____

_____

_____

_____

_____

_____

_____

_____

*"Don't you quit…don't you dare quit!"*

*"If you say you can't you aint"*

*"Aint, never done nothing."*

*"It doesn't matter how big the door; the question
is do you have the key to open the door?"*

*"If you caught it do something with it!"*

*"Don't settle."*

*"Your success is not predicated upon who is for or against
you; your success is up to you because it is within you."*

*"The outward appearance looks good, well
packaged but what about the heart?"*

*"If you are limited in the mind, you limit your life line."*

*"You don't have to be smart to be gifted."*

Personal Journal

_____
_____
_____
_____
_____
_____
_____
_____
_____
_____
_____
_____
_____
_____
_____
_____
_____
_____
_____
_____
_____
_____
_____

*"You are not responsible how people treat you but
you are responsible how you treat people."*

*"So what if you are starting over again
hey… at least you started!"*

*"Thoughts can help you go forward or they
can set you back…You choose."*

*"Be true."*

*"How long will it take to be missed, when you are missing?"*

*"It's not about the one dragging along trying to hold on
it's about that same one trying to pull you back."*

*"It may be a struggle but it will pay off."*

*"When you throw dirt… it may be thrown back at you."*

Mr. Brown's Sunday School Class

*"Many want to preach but they aren't preaching what is relevant to the times."*

Jonathan Rice

*"Some people are doing ...what they gotta do what they must do... what they need to do... what they should do. Some are doing absolutely nothing. What are you doing?"*
Brenda Rice

Personal Journal

_____
_____
_____
_____
_____
_____
_____
_____
_____
_____
_____
_____
_____
_____
_____
_____
_____
_____
_____
_____
_____
_____
_____

*"Most of the time if you love people, people will love you back."*

*"If you play you will pay!"*

*"No train can go where tracks have never been laid."*

*"You have to prove it if you want to earn it!"*

*"Do what you gotta do to get what you
gone get!" (Do what's right)*

*"Sometime you might get a signal and sometime you may not."*

*"It is necessary that the younger listen to
the older." (advice that helps)*

*"You can't witness what you did not witness."*

*"A dream fulfilled brings life. A dream unfulfilled brings despair."*

*"Well-do!"*

◊

*The battle is the Lord's!! But the victory is mine!!"*

◊

*"I will ask you but I'm not gonna beg."*

◊

*"It is better to get there safely than not to get there at all."*

◊

*"Set your expectations high and operate from that level of expectancy."*

◊

*"When you give…you will get it back."*

◊

*"If you don't know nothing then don't say nothing."*

*"Think before you act."*

Personal Journal

_____
_____
_____
_____
_____
_____
_____
_____
_____
_____
_____
_____
_____
_____
_____
_____
_____
_____
_____
_____
_____
_____
_____
_____
_____

*"Losing but gaining."*

*"Working hard to obtain and maintain,
completing the task we started."*

A Day's Work

*"Talk love all you want to but if you don't
show it, I start wondering."*

*"Raised hell for the devil…Why stay quiet for God?"*

*"The one we think God won't use is the one he will use."*

*"You need people around you that will build
you up and not break you down."*

*"Don't measure down!!!!! Measure up!!"*

*"If our mansions were built based on praise some
of our mansions would look like shacks."*

*"A woman of peace and a woman of war."*

*"You can't link up with everybody and
bring them into your life."*

*"You can sting like a bee and still be sweet as honey."*

◊

*"Don't allow negative thoughts in your mind 'cause it takes too much energy to get them out."*

◊

*"You really will be better off thinking on whatz good!"*

◊

*"I am not where I'm going but I'm on my way... I'm on my way somewhere!!!!!!!!!"*

◊

*"Don't let life pass you by."*

◊

*"Your life can be heard...without saying one word."*

◊

*"Sometime all it takes is a smile."*

*"Many were praying but weren't watching
and the devil took them by surprise."*

*"Keep speaking you broke and you will be broke."*

*"A boy with a man's mentality."*

*"Victory comes with a price!"*

*"Even when you are not obligated use
it as an opportunity to be a blessing."*

*"I am glad I don't have to wait 'til
Sunday to get my breakthrough!"*

"The one that trys to get rid of you; God will get rid of them."

"Don't be bound!"

"…I got a praise that I cannot hold!!!"

"God is the way made!"

"You don't have to ever fight folks who want to stop you from completing your assignment…God will fight for you!!!"

"Be a gap filler not a fence holder."

"The course is set now you set the pace."

"God doesn't need spectators He needs participators."

*"A small boy with big faith."*

TAKING A PEEK
By Tiffany Taylor

> "I *will be found guilty for using the gifts and talents God has given me…*Are *you?*"
>
> Brenda Rice

Personal Journal

_____

_____

_____

_____

_____

_____

_____

_____

_____

_____

_____

_____

_____

_____

_____

_____

_____

_____

_____

_____

_____

_____

_____

*"Don't quit!!!!!Don't you dare quit!!!"*

*"Judge no man before hand."*

SERENITY
By Tiffany Taylor

*"Everything is good!"*

Personal Journal

_____
_____
_____
_____
_____
_____
_____
_____
_____
_____
_____
_____
_____
_____
_____
_____
_____
_____
_____
_____
_____
_____
_____

*"Have a Bless one!"*

# I Speak Blessings

*May the Lord bless you and keep you,*
*may the Lord make His face to shine upon you and*
*be gracious to you; may the Lord lift up His countenance*
*upon you, and give you peace. May God bless you and enlarge*
*your territory; may the hand of God be with and keep you*
*from harm so that you will be free from pain.*
*And these blessings will come upon you and*
*accompany you if you obey the Lord your God;*
*wherever you go, wherever you are, you will be blessed.*
*Wealth and riches shall be in your house. He*
*will bless them that fear him both small and great.*
*May the Lord increase you more and more, you and*
*your children. You are blessed of the Lord.*
*May your seed be mighty in the earth: the*
*generation of the upright shall be blessed. May*
*you prosper and be in health even as your*
*soul prospers. May the Lord bless you in all you do; your*
*harvest and all the works of your hand. May the Lord open the*
*windows of heaven and pour you out blessings you won't have*
*room to receive. May you trust in the Lord with your heart and*
*lean not on your own strength. May you*
*delight yourself in the Lord and*
*he will give you the desires of your heart.*
*May you commit your way*
*unto the Lord and trust also in Him to bring*
*it to pass. May you rest in the Lord*
*and wait patiently for him and he will grant*
*you your desires. May you always*

*bring honor, glory and praise to the Lord*
*who is the creator of all things in*
*Heaven and Earth! I SPEAK BLESSINGS!!*

*God bless,*
Brenda T. Rice

### *Special Thanks*

*Thank you so much for purchasing a copy of this book.
All proceeds will provide financial support for the mission
ministry as I travel locally, in the United States and
internationally. It gives me the opportunity to share the
message of hope and inspiration to many. It is my strong
desire to make a difference as I touch one life at a time in
my own community, towns and villages of other nations.*

*God Bless You,*
Minister Brenda T. Rice


*Nation to Nations*

> *"Praise God!!!*
>
> *What was only a dream conceived…*
> *is now my reality!!!!!!"*
>
> Brenda Rice

**Contact Information: Email:** brend_song@yahoo.com

**Brenda T. Rice P.O. Box 1932 Henderson, N.C. 27536**